DARE TO MAKE A DIFFERENCE

SUCCESS 101

JOHN A. ANDREWS

NATIONAL BESTSELLING AUTHOR

Published in the U.S.A. by
BooksThatWillEnhanceYourLife.com

A L I
Andrews Leadership International
www.AndrewsLeadershipInternational.com

Cover Design: John A. Andrews
Cover Photo: Anthony Johnson
Edited by: Teen Success

DARE TO MAKE A DIFFERENCE

SUCCESS 101

This book is dedicated to those who have patiently held up the ladder for me. How their hands must have calloused and ached. To my mother, a true legend, Elaine Louisa Andrews, who lived a life of dedication and service to her church and community. To my dad who passed when I was nine. To my three sons: Jonathan, Jefferri and Jamison. And to the numerous leaders, who've invested in me thereby impacting my life.

Losers let things happen, but winners make things happen. Winners are never satisfied with who they are, and therefore, they're constantly working on changing and enhancing their self-image. They have a vision of the person they want to become, and they develop a well-defined, emotional picture of themselves, as if they have already achieved that goal. Advance winning pumps through winners' veins.

- They breathe the championship.

- They feel drenched from the entire bucket of Gatorade poured over their head.

- They experience the thrill of Disneyland before playing the Super Bowl.

- They caress the Oscar.

- They hear the crowd's approval.

- They feel the gold medal around their neck.

- They see a church with 1 million members worshiping in spirit and truth.

- They stand tall in the winner's circle.

- They feel their new self-image in advance.

- They dress rehearse receiving the Nobel Prize.

Winners let nothing stand in the way of victory. You can smell their tenacity like expensive cologne because they have a feeling of their own worth. They think, "I can. I will, and I shall not be denied."

Our deepest fear is not that we are inadequate.
Our deepest fear is that we are powerful beyond measure.
It is our light, not our darkness that most frightens us.

We ask ourselves, who am I to be brilliant, gorgeous, talented and fabulous?
Actually, who are you not to be?
You are a child of god. Your playing small doesn't serve the world.

There's nothing enlightened about shrinking so that other people won't feel insecure around you.
We were born to make manifest the glory of God that is within us.
It's not just in some of us, it's in everyone.

And, as we let our own light shine, we unconsciously give other people permission to do the same. As we liberated from our own fear, our presence automatically liberates others.[1]

- Marianne Williamson

Contents

Introduction

For what do I want to be remembered? This is a fundamental question asked by just about every successful individual. Because like the caterpillar going through the cocoon to become a beautiful butterfly, equally, all truly victorious people go through walls, which stood in their way towards their destiny. They will also tell you that their success principles were rooted, deep down, inside of them and were the defining elements which helped create the success that you see all around them. If you nurture those roots which run deep within you, your chance of succeeding is inevitable.

In 2009 Senator Barack Obama was elected as Americas' first black president. Obama, who rose to great success, grew up during the civil rights revolution of the 1960s, when blacks were not permitted to ride in the front of the bus as whites did, dine in certain restaurants or even permitted to vote. In that era "segregation" was not only an academic institutional slogan, but rather an uncomfortable household word to the Negro race. The fundamental reason, back then severe limits were placed on the associations of these two races - with blacks at a stringent disadvantage. Obama went through those walls and consequently, earned the American vote.

During that civil rights era of intense racial conflicts, leaders such as Malcolm X and Dr. Martin Luther King Jr. emerged on the scene. King, a black man from the south fought for, and lost his life (assassinated) daring to fulfill his dream of equality. A dream that: One day his children would not be judged by the color of their skin but by the content of their character.2. In addition: that one day all children regardless of the color of their skin would live together in unity. [3]

In 1969 a school teacher by day and an insurance agent by night from Oklahoma City was involved in an automobile accident a head on collision. His car got totaled as a result. The police officer called to the scene cited the other driver, a woman, at fault. She later sued Mr. Harland Stonecipher. He was not only hospitalized, but he exhausted his life savings of almost $4,000.00 defending himself against that lawsuit. He ended up winning but felt as though he had lost. In today's economy that amount of money would equal almost $40,000.00.

Consequently, he searched not only the U.S but also Europe and found out that most Europeans owned a legal plan in order to protect their rights. He adopted the concept and brought it to America, and at this moment in time almost two million families have access to top quality advice whenever they need it for just over a dollar a day. Because of this adversity, his destiny in the present climate embodies a two-fold mission. (1) To provide equal justice under the law for all North American families. (2)To create more millionaires than any other company has ever created in history.4

Oprah Winfrey was born in Mississippi at a time when segregation in that state denied basic civil rights to African Americans. She came from a home with no electricity and drinking water, also a victim of a troubled youth. As a child she was required to read books and every two weeks, to write a report about what she had read. Oprah would often say that she wanted to make her living by talking. She was a gifted, quick-witted speaker.

In 1972 she became the first black woman to hold the anchor position at Nashville's WTVF-TV. In 1986 she launched the Oprah Winfrey Show. In 1994 she bought her own studio "Harpo." In 1996 she began Oprah's book club to promote reading, for which she recommends a recently published book each month. She sets aside one show each month for a full discussion on the book. She has since created her classic book club, which features three authors per annum. Oprah regularly gives 10% of her income to charities, mostly having to do with youths, education and books.

Oprah Winfrey, who became a billionaire at age 49, has not only risen to become the most powerful and influential woman in the television world but ruler of a large entertainment and communications empire - from a life of poverty and abuse to a life of greatness. Oprah Winfrey at one point in her broadcast career believed in herself so much, sources close to her knew that she was like a hit record to be released. It wasn't long before she became that hit record. She has broken down so many walls. Now when she talks - people absolutely listen.

Pastors Philip and Holly Wagner resides in Los Angeles, California. I first met them in 2001 at the Oasis Christian Center. Holly is a former actress. Philip is a pastor's kid came from a home of devout Baptists. Born in the sixties Philip could not escape racial injustice seen firsthand by his parents. Together they started the church at a home bible study in Beverly Hills, with 10 people in attendance. This grew to about 60 people, and then declined week by week. In those early years, they would tell you that they struggled with their relationship. After 24 years this church, situated in the heart of Hollywood currently resembles the United Nations because of its many diverse tonicities in attendance and has in this day and age grown to over 2,000 members strong.

Today the church not only quenches the spiritual thirst of many Southern Californians but supports several mission outreach programs around the world.

Philip was very instrumental in the creation of "Generosity Water" an organization which gives 100% of its profits towards building water wells in Uganda and other countries around the world. That organization has now helped to build over 50 water wells for Ugandan residents.

In fulfilling their destiny, Philip and Holly have not only removed the walls of racism and social injustice but have also taught many relationship seminars around the world while they're constantly working on theirs.5.

Is your destiny a cause greater than self? Is it a life of boundlessness?
There are things you and I will accomplish in our lifetime that will not only astonish our relatives, friends, neighbors, co-workers but our enemies alike. It has been discovered that 90% of an iceberg

rests beneath the surface. It may surprise you that each of us has at least 90% of our potential lying untapped. As human beings we are known to use only that other 10% of our potential.

In my interaction with successful people from all walks of life, I have discovered that they are not only specialists in their field, but that they had at one point in their lives said yes to their potential. In my journey up the ladder of success, I've learned to become "a sponge" by learning from them; I've worn their shoes, and felt some of their pain. You will meet most of them as well as me through these pages. Most of all because success leaves clues, you will discover that as human beings, they recognized their value, believed in their value, increased their value. Consequently, they've become valuable. Our world has been searching for you. It needs people who are willing to step off the sidelines and into the game. It needs individuals to make a significant difference.

I DARE YOU TO ACHIEVE SOMETHING THAT WILL MAKE THE FUTURE POINT TO YOU WITH EVEN MORE PRIDE THAN THE PRESENT IS POINTING TO THOSE WHO HAVE GONE BEFORE YOU.[1]

-WILLIAM DANFORTH

Chapter One

YOU!

In his book, The Genius Machine author Gerald Sindell asks: "How can you get out of your own ocean to see what differentiates you?"[2] Based on the worlds populous of almost seven billion people, you stand out. You might reason – Really? Me? That's impossible. I am nobody. I don't have the brains. I am from the wrong side of the tracks I don't have what it takes. I am not the best tool in the shed. I am not. I am not, and I am not. If you are holding onto those false beliefs about yourself – Understand, they are nothing but figments of your imagination.

Whenever you view any collection of photographs or a photo album, there's that human tendency to look double to see if you are included in those pictures, you look initially for yourself, even if you were not part of the photo shoot. Furthermore, if you were to, with time permitting check out the entire world's population, you won't find anyone exactly like you, including anyone with your peculiar abilities, intelligence or viewpoint. Have you ever pondered and come to the realization that there's a reason why you are the only one with your voice, thumb print along with many other attributes?

You may not believe it, comprehend it or even yet decipher it. Even so, if I were to tell you that you have the power within you to become successful: **A force which is at this moment in time, dormant.** When discovered and aroused, it will lift you from failure to success - A power which will dramatically transform you into a person of tremendous influence and success. And what if I were to tell you that all you have to do was to trust your power by knowing yourself? In his book On Becoming a Leader Warren Bennis writes: [Know thyself, then, means separating who you are and who you want to be from what the world thinks you are and wants you to be.[3] It is often said that "knowledge is power."

Self knowledge subsequently is your first key to success. See, if you seriously, I propose, genuinely get acquainted with you, and understand that the sky is the limit to your potential, you may not be able to go to sleep tonight. Captivated by such a burning desire to tap into that 90% unused potential which remains unleashed, you'd be wide awake planning the next series of moves for your life.

In addition if I were to tell you that by believing in yourself, breaking of old failure habits, changing your negative associates who've been constantly holding you back, and developing a sense of passion and purpose towards fulfilling your destiny. Would you, in exchange for a better, fuller and richer life step up to the plate?

YOU must realize that you're different. You are unique. You are beauty-fully and wonderfully made. When God made you, he completely destroyed the formula. He must have jubilantly said to his angels "There can never be another you! Some may try to imitate you, but it's a futile battle. You can never, never, be recreated." You are here, right now, and no one can be you but you. Be excitingly thankful for who you are as well as who you can become.

Imagine what would have happened if your mom had swung a little to her left or your dad had swung a little to his right. Result? - Missed target. Someone besides you eventually would have made it to this world. Those million plus tiny sperm cells racing through that dark alley to impregnate that patiently waiting egg, would have eagerly decided someone else's conception.

Unfortunately, and tragically, as human beings we place very little value on ourselves and subsequently acclimatize toward failure. We live in a world bombarded with negative news, pessimism and a failure mindset. As a result, devaluing ourselves has become such an easy thing to do. Watching Constant Negative News for a few hours over a period of time and we are hooked, immersed in all that negativity. As the saying goes, "garbage in garbage out." You hear and watch so much violence, now you're even afraid to go outside. Besides, you've not merely become fearful of others, but also you fear your own potential. Resulting in living your life with your light hid under a bushel.

As a responsible individual on your way to the top, realize that you are always looking at two different walls. You'll find that one says you are a top notch, and you can do whatever you can think, want or desire. The other says: You have no capital. You are uneducated. You don't have the energy it takes. You have failed before. You are too old. You are too young. You lack talent and abilities. You are too short, too tall. Too - everything. You are too ill-equipped succeed in life.

Conversely, when it comes down to causing a change, everything starts with you. You are in the driver's seat. You call the shots You are the captain of your row boat. You are the pilot of your aircraft. You set your own pace. Most of all you are the only handicap you must encounter towards your destiny. You chose success or failure – both learned vocations. The ball is in your hands – you dribble, or you shoot. When it all comes down to it if you miss, there's no one else to blame.

Any individual bent on success must eliminate the blame game completely from his or her mindset in order to have success. He focuses on his destiny. By doing so he develops the morale that "It's all or nothing." He eats, lives and breathes success. Thereby - creating war on any vice, which has kept or will keep him captive. With such a mindset, stepping out of his comfort zone becomes an embracing challenge. Consequently, this move, results in a much richer and rewarding lifestyle. In my book When the Dust Settles - I am still standing.

I referred to the story about the baby elephant chained to a stake, and after several years later, with the chain removed from its feet, conversely that elephant refused from setting itself free. Living such a life tied our circumstances - is a shell we must crack if our advancing is going to be inevitable.

Breaking yourself free and being all you can will take some effort. I am always reminded of the story of two men waiting at the dock. One man looked like he has been waiting there forever, putrid and un-kempt, smoking a cigarette. A ship pulled up, dropped that huge piece of iron to anchor. An agile man boarded, and while doing so, glanced at the dormant man and remarked, "Good to see you again, pal." Then he jumped aboard the ship. Before setting sail, he asked the waiting man: "What are you waiting for pal? I see you here all the time…" The man responded: "My ship, of course" as he lit up another cigarette continuing his chain smoking interlude. The man on the now sailing ship retorted, "Did you send one out? "No" he replied as he took a brisk puff on his cigarette releasing some ash. "Sorry, you have to send one out." He yelled back from his swiftly moving ship.

So many are waiting for their ship to come in when they never sent one out. They anticipate receiving without first giving. They are always looking for that someone to hand them something. A film producer of mine has experienced a growing movie franchise, generating over $100,000,000 with the last five yearly installments. Failures, looking at his success say he was lucky. I have known him over ten years and consider him as someone with a tremendous work ethic. Before his big break five years ago I'd seen him reading a screenplay after a screenplay and a novel after a novel looking for the right one. I've even handed him scripts noticing his passionate appetite.

One day before his big Christmas, my sons and I paid him a visit. He asked if we could watch his son play in the backyard while he caught up on his script reading, I obliged. In addition, I worked as an actor in a movie which he produced starring actor Denzel Washington and saw him engrossed in a novel which he read during the lunch break. An acquaintance of mine additionally told me that one day he saw him on an airplane with over six scripts in his briefcase. Today he is one of the top independent producers in Hollywood, and relishes a phenomenal lifestyle, one to be greatly desired.

In reading this volume on Success 101 mindset and philosophy, you will find that in order to go up you've got to grow up. Therefore, working on self takes precedence. In order to become a beautiful butterfly the caterpillar needs to go through the cocoon. By doing so, it can at this point fly from a tree to another tree pollinating them in the process, instead of feeding on a lonely tomato plant for survival during its pre-cocooned stage. The power that lies within that beautiful butterfly promptly enriches vegetation.

Each of us has talents and abilities lying dormant in us, mainly because we don't have the courage to dig them up and put them to use. Many times during conversations, people who know me as an author often mention that they want to write a book or have started writing a book but have never finished it. I normally respond with, "If you really want to do it, tonight before you go to bed embark on the process of creating the outline or dust off the computer's keyboard and continue writing. How many of them do it? I can tell you few dare.

In the book, I Dare You author William Danforth writes, I dare you to achieve something that will make the future point to you with even more pride than the present is pointing to those who have gone before you.[1]

Success is a journey. Though some like to think it's a destination. The people who continue to succeed value themselves and therefore, are not satisfied with who they are. They are constantly working on changing and enhancing their self image. They feel as though they have not scratched the surface in their chosen endeavor. They realize that success is all about the hustle, and dares anyone to outwork them. In essence, their life has to be a worthwhile endeavor. That championship, the super bowl, the bestseller, the Oscar, the crowd's approval, the gold medal, the one million church members in attendance, and receiving of the Nobel Prize. Those are all great accomplishments, yet those high achievers are not at all satisfied. They see the world as if it's a complex jig saw puzzle, and they are the missing piece towards the solution. They think, "If it's going to be fixed - it's up to me."

It doesn't matter who you are, where you are, where you live, what you have or don't have, who your parents are. If you dare to cause that change, you have enlisted yourself in a great cause that will certainly bless humanity beyond your imagination.

YOU no doubt by reading this book had already defined yourself. If you are not ready for your own success, feel free to pass this volume on to someone else desiring all they had ever wanted to become. However, if you have a burning desire to go through the wall standing in your way for far too long? If you care enough to succeed massively - your SUCCESS is inevitable!

"IF AN ORGANIZATION DOESN'T HAVE A CLEAR PURPOSE AND SENSE OF WHAT BUSINESS IT'S IN, WE THINK THERE'S SOMETHING WRONG. YET FEW PEOPLE HAVE A CLEAR SENSE OF THEIR LIFE'S PURPOSE. HOW CAN YOU MAKE GOOD DECISIONS ABOUT HOW YOU SHOULD USE YOUR TIME IF YOU DON'T KNOW WHAT BUSINESS YOU'RE IN?" [1]

- KEN BLANCHARD.

Chapter Two

PURPOSE

In the book, The Purpose Driven Life, Rick Warren writes: "Living on purpose is the only way to really live. Everything else is just existing."² Too many of us drift along with the wrong crowd going nowhere fast. In The Master Key To Riches author Napoleon Hill recounts a statement by Andrew Carnegie, the man who developed a fortune by going the extra mile: "The person who is motivated by definiteness of purpose and moves on that purpose with the spiritual forces of his being may challenge those who are indecisive at the post and pass them at the grandstand. It makes no difference whether someone is selling life insurance or digging ditches."³ It's a known fact that physically and mentally lazy people tend to remain in their comfort zone far too long. At that place, no more growth ever occurs. Therefore, they never fully realize the good they often might win by stepping out. Subsequently, purpose remains unsupported or in most cases undefined. They fail in that effort to grow and stretch.

We live in a world full of half-alive people who are no longer sold on themselves. Any professional body-builder would tell you that a muscle only grows when it's stretched. The sleeping giants within you, needs to be awakened. James Allen states in As a Man Thinketh: Those who have no central purpose in life fall an easy prey to petty worries, fears, troubles and self pitying, all of which are indications of weakness, which lead just as surely as deliberately planned sins (though by a different route) to failure, unhappiness, and loss. For weakness cannot persist in a power-evolving universe. We should conceive of a legitimate purpose in our hearts and set out to accomplish it.4

There's a war to be fought - YOURS! Yes, lifting your head up above the crowd will give you purpose, ammunition and direction in life. You will see where you need to go. And the world always seems to make a way for the person who knows where he or she is going. Streets are crowded; a fire engine is coming through. Everything gives way, pedestrians, vehicles, everything. They all step aside for this speeding machine on a mission. Why? It has a purpose – putting out the fire, and it has a sense of urgency in doing so.

THE CHAMPION

The average runner sprints

Until the breath in him is gone

But the champion has the iron will

That makes him "carry on.

For rest, the average runner begs

When limp his muscles grow

But the champion runs on leaden legs

His spirit makes him go.

The average man's complacent

When he does his best to score

But the champion does his best

And then he does a little more.

• Author unknown

A purpose driven individual will readily discover within that extra-ness necessary to overcoming all odds. The words "I can't" are totally eliminated from his or her vocabulary. Whenever he's confronted with any sign of defeat he resolves: "I am not giving up, bring it on. It might have licked some but not me. I absolutely will not be denied." Author Julia Cameron writing in her book The Artist's Way says, "I have learned, as a rule of thumb, never to ask whether you can do something. Say, instead, that you are doing it. Then fasten your seat belt. The most remarkable thing follows."5 Additionally she states, "Take a small step in the direction of a dream and watch the synchronous doors flying open." A maxim worth remembering, Leap, and the net will appear.6

That door, one day opened for director Steven Spielberg. He visualized making a unique film. With the script already in possession he needed a producer to finance it. One day while he was walking on the beach, he encountered a man who not only had the resources but was willing to invest in young film makers. This total stranger stepped up to the plate and gave Spielberg the money, enabling him to shoot Amblin. That film was given an honorable mention at the Venice Film Festival and opened the door for him coming to Hollywood. The rest is history.[7]

When we know what we want and embark upon accomplishing it, amazing things occur. Let's visit with some purpose driven individuals who no doubt will take away the excuses of many.

Human Activist, Helen Keller could have said "Me? I was born blind and deaf."

Inventor, Thomas A Edison could have said "Who needs an incandescent light bulb? I have already tried 10,999 times."

Steve Jobs, the founder of Apple computers, could have said "I'm way too young to achieve massive success." He made his first million at age twenty-three, his first ten million at twenty-four, and at age twenty-five his first 100 million.

President Abraham Lincoln could have said "I am a big failure politically. I have already lost eighteen elections. I would never become the American president."

President, Nelson Mandela could have said "My own countrymen threw me in jail, where I've spent most of my life. I could never become the president of my country.

Colonel Sanders, the founder of Kentucky Fried Chicken could have said "I dropped out of high school, plus I 'm way over 40 - way too old to succeed in life." He didn't fulfill his dream until age 65 and received 1,009 "NO'S" before he got a "YES."[8]

Paul Getty, the world's first billionaire could have said "I'm not born a businessman. I have no business being in business." Yet he became a model for some of the most successful business people of our time. Getty said "I'd rather have 1 % of the efforts of a hundred men than 100% of my own efforts."[9] He owns the Getty Museum in Los Angeles, California. One of my associates, about these huge landmark remarks: "Getty owns a mountain and that's the only man I know to do so."

President, John F. Kennedy could have said "I am too young to become the American president; no one is going to listen to me."

President, Truman could have said "I have not once attended college. I could never become president of America."

Artists, Ray Charles and Stevie Wonder could have said "we are blind, how are we going to find the keys to the piano, besides, sing to an audience which we cannot see?"

Charlie Chaplin, one of history's wealthiest actors could have said "I grew up in poverty roaming the streets of London. I'll never amass a fortune."

Astronaut, Neil Armstrong could have said 'The moon is so out of reach I have no business going up there."

[Most people lack the initiative needed in order to become all they were meant to be, mainly because they don't believe, deep down, inside that they are valuable] Therefore, they live with a purpose deprived life. Purpose, a directive word, which means heading towards something, gains momentum when meshed with the propellant word belief – that feeling knowing that you can do whatever you set out to do. People, lacking the propellant in themselves usually look for this additive coming from someone else, and when they don't receive it, they wonder why their life spins around like a tap in mud – going nowhere fast. In order to take advantage of others believing in you, you must first harness the power of belief in yourself.

When a commercial airplane is getting ready for takeoff, first the doors are closed shut. Passenger's seat belts are securely fastened. The plane then taxis down the runway in preparation for takeoff. The Air Traffic Controllers in the tower sees that the plane is ready for takeoff. Instruction is then given to the pilot to speed up. He releases the throttle, retracts the landing gear and engages the skies.

Believing in you will initiate purpose. Belief: that ability necessary to taxi down the runway in your preparation for takeoff. As soon as others start believing in you, your takeoff becomes eminent. Mark 9:23 states, All things are possible to him who believes. Successful people believed that they were going to be victorious and sat sail in pursuit of their objective. Their lives became driven by the desire to succeed. They knew where they were going and consequently, found their hidden guides to take them there.

As an immigrant to the United States several years ago, I sensed that Americans are so fortunate because of the many opportunities, which exist in this country, and that they often take their heritage for granted.

Conversely back then I felt like the odds were stacked against me, coming from the Caribbean and not being able to master the Standard American

English. Nevertheless, I've learned to grasp those opportunities which could lead me to the next level.

Consequently, some amazing people have stepped into my life as guides, including my mentor and friend Bob Wilson. He had just retired after teaching elementary and high school teacher for a period of 35 years. We originally met when he played my Dad in a student film - the adaptation of Guess Who Is Coming To Dinner. This was my initial film project when I moved to Hollywood in 1996. He has always guided me back on the right path, especially during those early years of my divorce, and has played the role of a devil's advocate on numerous occasions. Addition-ally, Bob has helped me to validate my belief in myself, as I dare to make a difference Bob has an amazing intuitive spirit.

Belief in self is paramount if there is ever going to be any worthwhile accomplishment. Remember, no one else really believes in you until you first believe in yourself. If an organization doesn't have a clear purpose and sense of what business it's in, we think there's something wrong. Even so, few people have a clear sense of their life's purpose. How can you make good decisions about how you should use your time if you don't know what business you're in?[1] According to Ken Blanchard in Leading At A Higher Level.

Once you are airborne, then fasten-your-seatbelt signs extinguished, you are now not only committed to flying but at what speed. And most of all you know where you are going.

CHARACTER CANNOT BE DEVELOPED IN EASE AND QUIET. ONLY THROUGH EXPERIENCE OF TRIAL AND SUFFERING CAN THE SOUL BE STRENGTHENED, VISION CLEARED, AMBITION INSPIRED AND SUCCESS ACHIEVED.[1]

- HELEN KELLER

Chapter Three

PASSION

How driven are you towards becoming the success you were really meant to be? Some people live their lives in a lukewarm "whatever happens" state. Water is known to boil at 211 degrees and at 212 degrees turn to steam enough to push any locomotive. That extra one degree has propelled many from failure to amazing success.

You, no doubt by now has developed a sense of purpose. You have to. Alternatively, you definitely wouldn't be reading this far. However, do you have a sense of urgency to succeed? Already defined, you know why you exist and your destiny. Even so, permit me to rephrase. Do you have the zeal to make things happen? Without a burning desire, no one will see your readiness. There's plenty of room at the top but not too many are passionate enough about getting there. That's why they never arrive. They act as if they have forever to live and unfortunately the successful good life eludes them.

Everything that exists was first an idea acted upon either by you or someone else. As a writer I have met so many people with an idea for the next bestseller or the upcoming hit movie. Even so, they never write it. Consequently, their idea under no circumstances makes it to the book shelf or the screen. What would happen if you were told that you only have a month to live? How zealous would you be about getting things done? Would the back burner be empty or still filled with your dreams?

Some people like to watch things happen. Some people like to wonder what will happen, and some people don't really care what happens. However, the action-driven person delights in making things happen. Become branded for doing things. When you see something that ought to be done, step up to the plate and hit the home run. Once you acquire the action habit, others have no choice but to step aside for you. Take one step forward in the direction of your goals and dreams, and your enemies will run for cover. They see your value and hear the sirens.

In The 5 Steps To Changing Your Life, I also related a story about a young man who was working as a second hand on a railroad. His thoroughness subsequently won him an opportunity to work in a shipping office. During the interim, the substitute clerk asked this young buck for some facts and figures. The young man didn't know anything about bookkeeping, but he spent three days and three nights without sleep and had the facts ready for the superintendent when he returned. That passionate act of decision and commitment later propelled him into the vice-presidency seat of his own company.

Successful people make it a practice of getting things done while unsuccessful people are routine procrastinators. The successful person sees a great opportunity to go into business for himself while the unproductive person waits until that trend passes him by. He subsequently misses out on the opportunity to become a profiteer and resorts to the status of a consumer.

Bill, an associate of mine, who made his millions in Network Marketing, recounted to me this story. One day he took several of his top income earners on an island hopping expedition in the Caribbean. Enchanted by the pretty blue water they took to the seas. Many took that opportunity to show off their water skills. One associate, in particular, wanted so badly to rank advance and would not let him Bill out of his sight. As they swam together, the associate asked my fiend: "Bill, I have done everything you told me to do yet I have not advanced. What do I need to do?" Bill remained quiet for a while as he marinated on the question. The water got deeper and deeper. Finally, he grabbed the associate by his neck and pushed him under and held him there. The associate kicked and screamed, while filling up his lungs with water. Bill released him. He surfaced furious as ever, screaming while spitting out water, "Bill, what the heck you are doing, trying to kill me? I thought you were my friend." Bill responded: "You are my friend. I was only trying to answer your question. See, when you want to advance as much as you wanted to breathe just now - you will succeed."

Life lessons have taught me that the great opportunities are captured by those who attack not by those who wait. According to William Danforth, "Each fish that battles upstream is worth ten that loaf in lazy bays." He also writes, Deep down, in the very fibre of your being you must light an urge that can never be put out. It will catch this side of your life, then that side. It will widen your horizon. It will light up unknown reserves and discover new capacities for living and growing. It will become, if you don't look out, a mighty conflagration that will consume your every waking hour. And to its blazing glory a thousand other lives will come for light and warmth and power.[2]

In 975 Bill Gates dropped out of Harvard to pursue his career as a software designer. He later was joined by his colleague Paul Allen in the co-founding venture of Microsoft. It was rumored that Gates also showed the concept to two of his other colleagues who said no. Other sources claimed that Gates had a cot in his office that he slept on, night after night for several years when he was getting Microsoft off the ground. In 1980 Gates developed the Microsoft Disk Operating System (MS-DOS). And he successfully sold IBM on this new operating system.

By the 1990s Microsoft had sold more than 100 million copies of MS-DOS making the operating system the all-time leader in software sales.

Gates' competitive drive and fierce desire to win have made him a powerful force in business, but it also consumed much of his life. In the six years between 1978 and 1984, he took a total of only two weeks vacation. Even so, on New Year's Day 1994

Gates married Melinda French, a Microsoft manager, on the Hawaiian island of Lanai. His fortune at the time of his marriage was estimated at very close to seven billion dollars. By 1997 his net worth was estimated at approximately $37 billion, earning him the title of "richest man in America. His contributions really amaze me, as is often said, "To whom much is given much is expected."

Aside from being the most famous businessman of the late 1990s, Gates also has distinguished himself as a philanthropist. He and wife Melinda established the Bill & Melinda Gates Foundation, which focuses on helping to improve health care and education for children around the world. The foundation has donated $4 billion since its start in 1996. Recent pledges include $1 billion over twenty years to fund college scholarships for about one thousand minority students; $750 million over five years to help launch the Global Fund for Children's Vaccines; $50 million to help the World Health Organization's efforts to eradicate polio, a crippling disease that usually attacks children; and $3 million to help prevent the spread of acquired immune deficiency syndrome (AIDS; an incurable disease that destroys the body's immune system) among young people in South Africa. In November 1998 Gates and his wife also gave the largest single gift to a U.S. public library, when they donated $20 million to the Seattle Public Library. Another of Gates's charitable donations was $20 million given to the

Massachusetts Institute of Technology to build a new home for its Laboratory for Computer Science.

In July 2000 the foundation gave John Hopkins University a five-year, $20 million grant to study whether or not inexpensive vitamin and mineral pills can help save lives in poor countries. On November 13, 2000, Harvard University's School of Public Health announced it had received $25 million from the foundation to study AIDS prevention in Nigeria. The grant was the largest single private grant in the school's history. It was announced on February 1, 2001, that the foundation would donate $20 million to speed up the global eradication (to completely erase) of the disease commonly known as elephantiasis, a disease that causes disfigurement. In 2002 Gates, along with rock singer Bono, announced plans for DATA Agenda, a $24 billion fund (partially supported by the Bill and Melinda Gates Foundation) that seeks to improve health care in Africa.[3]

Although Gates' parents had a law career in mind for their son, he developed his early interest for computers, which turned into his passion, resulting in the Microsoft phenomenon. His philanthropic lifestyle continues to make a difference.

One December evening in 1955, a seamstress for a department store in Montgomery, Alabama boarded a city bus en-route to her home.

It was during the civil rights revolution, when blacks were exclusively permitted to sit at the back of a bus. She walked pass the "whites only" section towards the middle of the bus.

With frequent stops the bus filled up. The driver, a white man, noticed that more people of his race were still boarding. So he ordered the people in the seamstress Rosa Parks' row to move to the back of the bus. Apparently, they gave him a deaf ear. Frustrated, he barked at those black passengers. They all got up except for Rosa Parks.

Subsequently, this revolting against, passionate act, by Rosa Parks, fueled the already simmering civil rights movement with Martin Luther King at the helm. Consequently, she was arrested and sent to jail after a sheriff was called to the scene.[4]

Today in America, not only are blacks and other minorities permitted to vote but a black man now sits in the White House as our commander and chief.

Which situation could you change for the better if you dared to cause a change in the world?

In 2002 I made several phone calls for at least three weeks to find out who held the rights to a 1970s classic film which I so desperately wanted to remake. When I found the studio that did, a woman answered the phone. I told her that I would like to acquire the rights for the film. Her response was "sorry. We don't give up those rights to any third party." That ticked me off as I was so bent on remaking that movie.

Without hesitation, I called a writer friend who had his script already optioned with a major studio and asked if he'd be willing to help me write my pet project. See, after being denied those rights, I decided that I was going to write my own, and someday they'll come begging for it. My friend told me that because he was signed with a manager it would be impossible for him to collaborate writing a script with me. Anyway, he sent me templates for writing a screenplay.

I didn't know how to use a computer's keyboard accurately; I had never taken a typing class. Nonetheless, I embarked upon writing my script using my right hand calculating the use of each key while looking forward to seeing what was written on the screen. I wanted to write and did.

Later I showed one of my screenplays to a director I knew. He responded with an email stating that it was the worse screenplay he'd ever read, and that I should give it up. As if that wasn't enough he stated that I was a novice. I didn't write anything for over a week but subsequently returned to the drawing board and wrote like a maniac. About a year afterward I purposely sent him one of my scripts. A few days later my phone rang. It was him. "John how are you, mate?" "AWSOME" I replied. "Great work! Not too many people know how to write action thrillers. It's a tough genre. You have got the knack." "Thanks" I replied even more enthusiastically.

With a few screenplays written and more in the works, including my upcoming Hollywood Story, plus many books already published within the past two years, four of those in less than a year. I'm very passionate about what lies ahead. In the words of Helen Keller, Character cannot be developed in ease and quiet. Only through experience of trial and suffering can the soul be strengthened, vision cleared, ambition inspired and success achieved.

My typing style has not changed much since my writing debut. Even so, I refused from letting that temporary handicap fence me in with my vision sitting on the launching pad. I have decided to become unstoppable. I believe in a source greater than me and knowing that if the thought occurs, it can be written.

WHEN PEOPLE FEEL GOOD ABOUT YOU AND
THEMSELVES DURING THE TIMES THEY'RE
WITH YOU, THEN YOUR LEVEL OF INFLUENCE
INCREASES SIGNIFICANTLY.[1]

- JOHN MAXWELL

Chapter Four

PERSONALITY

Successful people always seem to exude that indescribable quality which attracts you to them like freckles of steel to a magnet. You feel it in their handshake, their pat on the back. You hear it in their intonations. They're looking you in the eye, and in their charismatic smile. They totally have "IT" and it's called personality. They draw you in. Indescribable, yet it moves you.

Where does personality come from? Is it something we are born with? Can it be developed? How do we get it? It can be acquired if you are willing to work on yourself.

Benjamin Franklin began as a printer's apprentice and later became the first self made millionaire in America. He adapted a process of personal development. As a young man he struggled realizing that he was somewhat ill mannered and argumentative, character traits which he realized was creating animosity toward him from his co-workers and associates as well. In an effort to change, he rewrote the script of his personality. Franklin began by making a list of what that ideal person should possess. He then concentrated on developing one virtue each week. Some of those thirteen virtues included: tranquility, moderation, resolution, humility, order and temperance. He practiced and worked hard at these virtues. As a routine he would practice one virtue each week, then two weeks, then three weeks, and then for a one month until it became a part of his character.

As a result he not only became one of the most popular personalities but also very influential as well. His influence played a very important role as an ambassador from the United States during the constitutional convention, when the constitution and the Bill of Rights for the United States was debated, negotiated and agreed upon.[5] By daring to working on himself, he made himself into a person capable of shaping the course of history.

Some people have a greater capacity for the character trait more than others. And this has a lot to do with their social upbringing. A child who is raised in a home where love reigns, where both parents' love for each other grow daily, exercises a deeper sense of love for others. That child because he or she is continuously reminded of being special, being loved and filled with potential, weighs in higher on the personality quotient. Conversely, the child who grows up in a home where love is lacking on the part of their parents, the kid who is regularly told that they are deficient in so many ways. If adolescents are not schooled in this particular area, they tend to come in lower on the personality quotient.

The people who've learned from their failures like Benjamin Franklin have been knocked down so many times that they not only embrace "getting back up" with a smile but embraced the adversity simultaneously, knowing that they will get back up, and you better watch out when they do. Successful people tend to turn "IT" on like magic. Their magnetism wins you over in a heartbeat.

I've always made it a habit to learn something from the personality of every successful person I've encountered. Most of all I've noticed and admired this special trait, which is a characteristic of great leadership - the ability to solve problems. Obstacles have no chance, at least not for long. They have that leaders' mindset.

When I first met Mr. Stoncipher, he greeted me with a firm handshake, and he conveyed in his "good to meet you" the message that "John the world needs you." That interaction spoke directly to my potential. That exchange gave such a tremendous boost to myself-esteem. How can I ever forget about my destiny whenever I associate with personalities like him?

Have you ever seen someone enter a room and immediately – charismatically – attract the warmth and attention of others? Understand, they were not born this way. One thing is for certain. They have become this way pursuant to their many failures along the way. They have learned how to laugh at, and amid their adversities. Personalities, who have made success their vocation, are like that whether you meet them on the top of a mountain or down in a valley. In good times or bad, they have the knack for attracting people.

These twelve traits speak volumes about an individual with an attractive personality.

1. He has conquered selfishness. Others have become his priority.

2 He knows that he'll reap what he plants. Therefore, his best gets sown.

3. He exercises self control.

4. He listens to others.

5. He gives with no strings attached

6. He recognizes the value in others.

7. He appreciates what others intend, not only what they do.

8. He lifts others up.

9. He's positive about life.

10. He leads and inspires others. When people leave his presence, they feel better about themselves.

11. He is a servant leader.

12. He keeps increasing his own value.

His leadership has influence. He lifts you to higher ground. Brian Tracy, in his book Million Dollar Habits writes: Make it a habit to go through life doing and saying the things that raise the self-esteem of others and make them feel valuable.[6]

In his book Becoming a Person of Influence John Maxwell writes: When people feel good about you and themselves during the times they're with you, then your level of influence increases significantly.[1] You now have a fresh outlook on life with a new feeling about yourself. And because it is easier for you to meet the needs of others once your needs have been met. You become a people magnet. Consequently, a domino effect is created causing others to win because you've won.

YOU WILL NEVER MAKE IT UPSTREAM WITH ONLY A MERE WISH. THE RAPIDS ARE FIERCE, THEY'LL PUSH YOU BACK DOWNSTREAM TOWARD SELF PITY AND MEDIOCRITY IF YOUR RESOLVE ISN'T STRONG ENOUGH.

Chapter Five

VISION

Where there is no vision the people perish, Proverbs 29:18 reads. That philosophy and mindset works without fail every time and is applicable to every area of a person's life. John F. Kennedy the youngest American president said this: "The problems of the world cannot possibly be solved by skeptics or cynics whose horizons are limited by obvious realities. We need men who can dream of things that never were."[1] No one succeeds without a vision. Let me explain: I am not talking about acquiring success without paying the full price, as in the case of someone winning the lottery. You may say what about receiving an inheritance, Isn't that luck? An inheritance is a good thing to leave behind, and I believe that every successful person should leave a legacy.

In the case of the lottery, players depend solely on luck of the draw. Unfortunately, that process has not put that winner through the mill of adversity to wind up with that lucky number; it was just mainly the purchasing of a ticket which produced that result. By now it should be fully understood that success is a learned endeavor, and self-made millionaires would attest to this. No lessons learned - no graduating. Success is not something you stumble into. It is a journey and inevitably as I've mentioned before - leaves clues. Wherever you focus your attention and put your energy, that area will bring forth fruit. As you sow, you will certainly reap.

Most people who have made the luck of the draw (the lottery), unfortunately are now penniless and lack the ability to recreate that kind of wealth. Mainly, because they have not gone through the growth process necessary to handle it.

When Henry Ford was asked what he'd do if he lost his fortune? He, without hesitation said that he would be a millionaire again within five years.[2]

Donald Trump, a self made billionaire at one point just about lost it all. However, because he had created most of his fortune, he could turn around and recreate it himself in a short space of time. He may have taken a detour but certainly not lost his direction.

It is often said that "if you don't know where you are going to any road will take you there." In the story about Alice In Wonderland, There was a point when Alice came to a fork in the road. She asked the Cheshire cat, "Would you tell me please, which way I ought to go from here?" The cat responded, "That depends a great deal on where you want to go." Alice told him that she didn't care much. The Cat smilingly gestured, "Then it doesn't matter which way you go." *Every vision needs to have a significant purpose. You need to know what you are doing and why. Then a picture of what it will be like once you arrive. No one wants to travel to a place without a beautiful end in mind. And what matters most are the values you take with you as your daily guide. It's important to enjoy the journey towards that particular destination.*[3]

Vision, the possibility of a dream coming true, moves us forward. There's something meaningful to wake up too – a journey to pursue. Peter Drucker said, "The best way to predict your future is to create it."[4] According to Ted Turner the creator of the broadcast empire, "A visionary is supposed to have a vision of the future."[5]

Howard Schultz, even if he wasn't the first person to be carried away by the aroma of a coffee bean. He saw potential in the espresso bar (Starbucks). Consequently, he convinced the owners to hire him. In 1982 they made him director of marketing. While on a trip to Italy he noticed that these coffee bars were not only on every block, but they served excellent espresso and served as meeting places at over 200,000 locations there.

Heading back to Seattle his plan of replicating met with huge resistance from the owners. His idea was rejected at least 250 times. Shultz, ticked off, started his own coffee business, called II Giomale. Pursuant to his successful venture, one year later he bought Starbucks for $3.8 million.

In addition to serving a great cup of coffee Schultz wanted to build a company with soul. So he insisted that all employees who work more than 20 hours a week get comprehensive health care coverage – included coverage for unmarried spouses. Additionally, they benefit from the employee stock option plan.

Schultz, also a lover of basketball, recently bought the Seattle Supersonics for $250 million.

When asked the secret of his success, he states four principles.

1. Don't be threatened by people smarter than you.

2. Compromise anything but your values.

3. Renew yourself when you are hitting home runs.

4. Everything matters.[6]

I'm always reminded of many childhood experiences, including watching my parents exercise their farming skills. First they prepared the land by removing the rough shrubbery. They plowed the land, and sowed corn in anticipation of a harvest. After a few days, the little corn plants sprouted. The corn was then watered and fertilized.

Weeds shot up attempting to destroy the now growing green acres of corn. My parents summoned us to embark on not only molding those plants but destroying the treacherous weeds. Like destroyers, we moved in hoeing with our hoe (an iron tool used to prepare the land and remove weeds). We whacked those weeds out and laid them to rot next to the corn plants - providing fertilizer for the now aggressively growing corn. It wasn't long before ears of corn were popping up everywhere. The birds came to get fed. We were once again summoned, and moved in with sticks which we inserted into the ground and tied black plastic bags to them. These served as a deterring object which as the wind blew chased the birds away.

It was in that present climate harvesting time as we picked numerous baskets of corn. My parents' vision was at that moment a reality as those ears of corn were sold on Friday's market. Not only that, we cooked, roasted, baked and ground corn for consumption.

Ken Blanchard writes, Vision generates tremendous energy, excitement, and passion because people feel they are making a difference. They know what they are doing and why.7 Successful people don't half step they see it BIG. They see opportunities where failures see a lack of. When a building is being demolished, they see more opportunities in the un-constructed edifice.

I attended an event about a year ago where Robert Kiyosaki was the keynote speaker. Robert in addition to talking about his rich dad poor dad philosophy based on his book Rich Dad Poor Dad addressed his prediction of the oncoming recession. Mr. Kiyosaki articulated the importance of accu-mulating wealth during its tenure and the fact that it would get much worse before it even gets better. The year 2008 has been a tough year for our country economically. It served up a compilation of huge company bailouts, bank mergers, layoffs, unemployment now in the millions, home foreclosures, the closing of several businesses, and the rising cost of health care as well gasoline.

Any economist will tell you that it's not yet over. They will also tell you that it is the worse it has ever been since the 1929-1939 depression, and the fact remains that we have not yet experienced the bottom of it all. In my opinion, if entrepreneurs and big thinkers don't step up to the plate it could be a long haul for many waiting to score financially.

What are the people with a failure mindset doing? Complaining, becoming cynical. Conversely, the visionaries buckle down and search for ways to create massive wealth. Why? It's a known fact that during a recession most people sell their possessions at huge discounts in order to survive. The cost of homes has declined drastically and continues to do so. In January of 2009, I was reading through a luxury home magazine, which I later loaned it to a friend. My friend subsequently picked out a home in Beverly Hills, California, for her vision board. At the time the home was listed at $12.5M.

A month later after church we decided to take a dream tour of it. The home was now going for $9.5M. I happen to know the seller who is a very successful Hollywood movie producer. He knew that if he didn't sell it quickly, in the next twelve months he could end up selling it for less than half of the initial list price. I returned a month later for a second tour. That house was already in escrow.

Chris Gardener had spent most of his childhood years shuffled between foster homes and other relatives, after his mother couldn't adequately support him and his other siblings any longer.

He also struggled to find his way after graduating high school. He later enlisted in the U.S. Navy with hopes of leaving the country. This dream of his never materialized.

After several odd jobs, earning sometimes less than $10,000.00 a year he met a stockbroker who drove a Ferrari plus earned over $80,000.00 a month. Enthused, he decided to become a stockbroker himself and went out persistently knocking on doors of investment firms hoping to find one that would give him a chance. Consequently, he found himself in jail after a police officer ran his license tags and discovered $1,200 of fines in unpaid parking tickets that he owed the city.

After 10 days in jail, he went directly to a job interview with Dean Witter – dirty jeans and all. The interviewer, after hearing his story, sympathized and hired him. Pursuant to that bold move on Chris' part, his bio has turned into one of the greatest success stories in American history.

During that interim, he lost his job. His ex-girlfriend left him to raise their 18 month child alone. He also got kicked out of his home. While studying for his broker exams, he lived in shelters and $10 a night motel with his son. Pursuant to his determination, he received his brokers' license and got hired by Bear Stearns. In addition his bio has made it to the big screen. And the rest is history for this man who kept looking forward.[8]

What are your visions for your future? What do you have listed on your dream board? Is it something that wakes you up out of bed excited with the zeal to dominate or do you approach it rather tentatively? Sean, an acquaintance of mine, now in his early 30s, was over $23,000.00 in debt and lived in a garage with his fiancé Loren, without a restroom seven years ago. He got involved in a home based business. On his dream board, he placed his dream car, a gray Mercedes Benz, a town house, a black and white pen along with other items.

Today, Sean has already earned close to a million dollars in passive income in addition to the gray Mercedes Benz, the town home which he totally gutted out and remodeled, and that black and white pen which he carries with him all the time. He'd hinted to me about his plan to surprise his bride on their wedding day. Last year I attended their dream wedding. In the middle of the ceremony he surprised her with the delivery of a gray hard top convertible BMW. He, an Israeli immigrant to the U.S. now enjoys spending most of his time with Loren while creating a vision for other entrepreneurs.

Humanity though sometimes anti-visionary never forgets its dreamers.

Columbus cherished the vision of another world, and he discovered it.[9] Although, some didn't help fund his expedition, and many others claimed that he was totally insane.

Copernicus fostered a vision of a multiplicity of worlds and a wider universe, and he revealed it.10

Henry Ford visualized, then designed and built his famous Model-T. And as a result, today we do not ride around on a horse and buggy.

Dr. Martin Luther King Jr. had a dream that black kids and white kids will hold hands together, and it has come to pass. To quote Dr. King: "If a man hasn't discovered something that he'll die for, he isn't fit to live."[11]

What visions do you have sitting on the back burner that you genuinely believe can never be accomplished? Dare yourself by bringing them forward! Dust them off! Write them down. You may be keeping accounts, and presently you shall walk out of the door that has for so long has seemed to be the barrier of your ideals, and shall find yourself before an audience-the pen still behind your ear, the ink stains on your fingers-and then and there shall pour out the torrent of your inspiration. You may be driving sheep, and you shall wander to the city-bucolic and openmouthed; shall wander into the studio of a great master And after a time the great master shall say, 'I have nothing more to teach you' And now you have become the master, who did so recently dream of great things while driving sheep. You shall lay down the saw and the plane to take on the regeneration of the world."[12] According to Stanton Kirkham Davis.

Our world needs men and women with vision, men who are willing to Man up. It also needs women with the tenacity of Rosa Parks.

A vision needs to be strong and unwavering; no one makes it upstream with just a mere wish. If you have a vision and think that you can't accomplish your vision, watch out because somebody else will.

Yikes! Tough statement but it's true. Someone else will eat your chocolate covered ice cream and smile while doing so.

THE WORLD-MUCH AS WE WANT IT TO BE-DOES NOT ACCORD WITH OUR INTUITION...THOSE WHO ARE SUCCESSFUL AT CREATING SOCIAL EPIDEMICS DO NOT JUST DO WHAT THEY THINK IS RIGHT. THEY DILIBERATELY TEST THEIR INTUITIONS.[1]

- MALCOLM GLADWELL

Chapter Six

TIMING

Timing is everything. The famous axiom states: The "T" in timing is better than the "T" in talent. As I mentioned previously if your mom and dad did swing inadvertently you would have ended up in "no man's land." If the sun misses it an appointment with planet earth we could for a long time be in utter darkness. If the waves miss their timing the ocean will swallow us up.

Timing has a lot to do with synchronicity but more so with preparedness. Successful people not only are adept at preparation. They rely on their intuition to capitalize on ideas. Therefore, whenever a great opportunity presents itself. They are all over it. Benjamin Disraeli says, "The secret of success in life is for a man to be ready for his time when it comes,"[2] Abraham Lincoln one of the biggest failures in life said: "Give me six hours to chop down a tree, and I will spend the first four sharpening the axe."[3] Let me rephrase in case you missed it, when one is prepared and the right opportunity presents itself, he seizes it and totally dominates. That's what others call luck. In my opinion, that is Success 101 – the way a high achiever performs.

High achievers love what they do and are at their best doing so. They allow their creativity to operate at the maximum. Conversely, many people allow their creativity to be caged up doing things they detest doing - simply because it pays the bills. I have seen people with so much potential waste it away behind a cubicle. They would rather be leveraged than leverage others. Many of the successful people I know today welcome business opportunities only if it has leverage. They want to know that they can build something and get paid continually whether they are able to perform or not. J. Paul Getty certainly understood this concept no wonder. He was the first recorded billionaire.

Today in America "leverage" the word of the wealthy has tremendous sex appeal. With so many layoffs people are beginning to realize that they need more than having a job. I believe that one of the blessings derived from this recession will be a major entrepreneurial revolution – producing more entrepreneurs than any other economic downturn in our nation's history. My prediction is that the people who make that switch by thinking outside of the cubicle will produce more wealth than many others who have gone before them.

I was recently introduced to Arri, a very ambitious man in his 30s. He made a huge fortune back in his college days in the pager business – way in the millions. At one point, he almost got kicked out of his dorm because of the constant flow of clients. He later sold that business to get into the cell phone business. Very few people owned a cell phone - somewhat of a two percentile did back then. He was smart enough to place himself in-front of that trend.

In that business, he made millions and sold it to get into the DSL business when the dial up was proven to be far to slow for graphics and the much larger files. He has also dominated in that industry. Arri thrives on picking the right opportunity at the right time – he positioned himself in-front of the trend rather than behind it.

Most successful people aren't lucky; they just master the law of timing. My movie producer friend amassed his fortune through a string of events. After his divorce, he later moved into an apartment complex managed by my ex-wife and me. He made his first big movie, which generated over $35M. It wasn't long before he moved out and bought a house in a fairly upscale neighborhood. When the idea for the horror film was presented to him by a struggling producer who was office-less and sometimes officiated from my friend's office couch.

My friend sold that property, put some money down on another and used a portion to finance the film. The film has grossed over $100M in its first and subsequent installments. He used his mind-sight instead of his eyesight when he purchased that piece of property. His initial investment has now brought him an excess of over $500,000,000, within the last five years. Some said that he was lucky. I don't believe in luck. I believe that real success occurs when preparedness and opportunity meet.

In his bestseller Rich Dad Poor Dad Investor and business man Robert Kiyosaki talks about being a professional investor. He claims that the number one key is to find an opportunity that someone else missed. He writes' "You see with your mind what others missed with their eyes."[4] Kiyosaki explains: A friend bought this run down an old house. It was spooky to look at. Everyone wondered why he bought it. What that man saw that we did not was that the house came with four extra empty lots. He realized that by going to the title company. After buying the house, the man tore it down and sold the five lots to a builder for three times what he paid for the entire property. As a result he made $75,000 for two months' work.[5] He further explains: Great opportunities are not seen with your eyes. They are seen with your mind. Most people never get wealthy simply because they are not trained financially to recognize opportunities right in front of them. [6]

As you strive to realize your vision, expect to be criticized and or called lucky. James Allen writes: *The thoughtless, the ignorant, and the indolent, seeing the apparent effects of things and not the things themselves, talk of luck, of fortune, and of chance. Seeing others grow rich, they say, 'How lucky they are!' Observing others become intellectual, they exclaim, 'How highly favored they are!' And noting the saintly character and wide influence of still others, they remark, 'How chance aids them at every turn!' They do not see the trials and failures and struggles which these people have voluntarily encountered in order to gain their experience; have no knowledge of the sacrifices they have made, of the undaunted efforts they have put forth, of the faith they have exercised, that they might overcome the apparently insurmountable and realize the vision of their heart. They do not know the darkness and the heartaches; they only see the light and joy and call it "luck," They do not see the long and arduous journey but only behold the pleasant goal and call it "good fortune." They do not understand the process but only perceive the result and call it "chance."[7]*

Having a vision provides the propellant or the belief to see it come true. However, there's always going to be the naysayer(s) who will tell you that you don't have what it takes to make it a reality. Sometimes, if it is a close friend or relative they will certainly remind you of those skeletons in your closet. You may excitedly launch your ship but understand that those winds and storms are going to come billowing against you. Trusting their possible caring attitude, you can make that mistake of lending a deaf ear to your unused capacity crying out within you saying "you can do it!" If success was a piece of cake everyone would be successful, then there wouldn't be a reason to go through the cocoon and change. Unsuccessful people remain out of sync with success, mainly because they resist change. Ask any winner and they'll tell you that: The major difference between successful people and unsuccessful people is successful people master the art of bouncing back from failure. They keep on keeping on.

Do you know someone who started something but fail to finish? I know so many would be authors who begin writing a book, yet they never finish. It under no circumstances makes its way out of their hard drive. They live a life of "if only I can, or I wish I did." Don't fall into that trap; it's always fully baited with excuses waiting for failures bent on quitting. Launch your dream and pursue it with reckless abandon. Harriet Beecher Stowe declared: "When you get into a tight place and everything goes against you, 'til it seems as though you could not hold on a minute longer. Never give up then, for that is just the place and time that the tide will turn."[8]

Back in my pre-writing days, I could have said "let that major movie studio keep their film, do whatever they want to do with it. In Hollywood, it's a rat race mindset anyway. I wasn't meant to be a writer in the first place. I came here only to act so I'll sit and wait for the auditions. No one wants to read about what I have to say. I'm a high school dropout and on and on… Instead it was perfectly timed, a blessing in disguise – I heeded that call to write. In the book, The Tipping Point Malcolm Gladwell states: The world-much as we want it to be-does not accord with our intuition...Those who are successful at creating social epidemics do not just do what they think is right. They deliberately test their intuitions.

If you were to interview the most successful people in the world, they would tell you that one of the keys to their overwhelming success is that they trusted their hunch. Yes, it's like fishing; they felt the nibble and tugged on the line. I believe that when God gives you a vision he also gives you the ability, and in his timing you'll certainly reach your destination if you persevere.

NOTHING IN THE WORLD CAN TAKE THE PLACE OF PERSISTENCE. TALENT WILL NOT. NOTHING IN THE WORLD IS MORE COMMON THAN UNSUCCESSFUL PEOPLE WITH TALENT. GENIUS WILL NOT. UNREWARDED GENIUS IS ALMOST A PROVERB. EDUCATION WILL NOT. THE WORLD IS FULL OF EDUCATED DERELICTS. PERSISTENCE, DETERMINATION AND HARD WORK MAKE THE DIFFERENCE.[1]

— CALVIN COOLIDGE

Chapter Seven

DETERMINATION

We've now come to one of the most important chapters in this book. This embodies the defining quality between people who succeed and the ones who don't. You know yourself. You have a purpose. You have developed the passion. You acquired a magnetic personality. You created a vision for your life and found the right time to launch it. You leave no road for retreat. In other words "you burn the ships" the bridge gets demolished. In Think and Grow Rich, Napoleon Hill recounts this story: A great warrior faced with a situation which made it necessary for him to decide, which ensured him success on the battlefield. This leader was about to send his armies against a powerful foe. Whose men fearfully out numbered his. He got busy and loaded his soldiers in boats, sailed to the enemy's country, unloaded soldiers and equipment. Then he gave the orders to burn the ships that had carried them. Addressing his men before the first battle, he said "You see the boats going up in smoke. That means that we cannot leave these shores alive, unless we win! We now have no choice-we win-or we perish!" They won.[2]

All successful people have in common this particular trait. They have learned how to develop the habit of perseverance towards setting and reaching their goals. Their "not giving up mindset and philosophy" separates them from the rest of the world. They know that without determination they will never arrive at their destination. So they persist in spite of the obstacles which were presented along the way.

In getting there, they certainly develop patience. That strong character trait necessary for dealing with all the falls they're about to take. They become masters of the art of getting back up when they get knocked down.

In order to succeed in today's world and cause a change one needs to not only learn from their failures but also from their successes. They ought to be able to look back at those diametrically opposed experiences and say: "This is what I did in order to succeed and this is what I've learned. This is what I did that caused me to fail and this is what I've learned from that."

Determination has a lot to do with robust faith. And faith is described as "the evidence of things not seen." It calls for a concentrated unwavering faith, one capable of removing mountains along the way. I moved to Hollywood, California in July 1996 as an actor. Within those first two years, I landed 9 TV commercials in a thirteen month span. However, I then experienced a journey dominated by failures. So copious that, constantly being beaten up by life in Hollywood led me to believe every seed I planted was killed by haters and industry pythons alike before they grew up much less bear fruit. Those play haters who delighted in nothing more than to see my dreams remain on the launching pad. The multiple dream killers who find delight in squeezing my dreams out of me. They had it coming. I decided that I was going to start believing in myself.

I knew where I came from and where I wanted to go. The boy from the islands of St. Vincent and the Grenadines, who, went to school at times without shoes on his feet. I had had enough and was going from here on to make a significant difference. What I touched had to turn to gold. Dare the ones who tried to stop me or get in the way. I was like a rhino coming through. Failure wasn't going to be an option. I was going through whatever stood in my way, en-route to my destiny.

I had written several screenplays as I mentioned before but had always wanted to etch my first book. I felt that I had unique stories to share. So, on January 21st, 2007 after having a heart to heart, a mind over matter interlude with my hidden guide and mentor the late Dr. Martin Luther King Jr. I took that tremendous leap of faith. As I looked at his picture several times, reflecting on what he stood for. If only I could do 20 % of what he stood for I'd be very happy. Releasing just one percent of my untapped potential could make a significant difference in the world.

While pondering my own legacy, I knew that I had not done enough for mankind and myself. I stared at MLK's quote: "Take the first step in faith. You don't have to see the whole staircase. Just take the first step."[3] For well over 30 minutes. Consumed by it and all that he stood for, I passionately outlined my first book, The 5 Steps to Changing Your Life.

My contribution towards changing mindsets at this point took center stage. If I could help to change the mindset and philosophy of one dream deprived individual, this world would become a better place. I reasoned.

So, through inspiration I was moved to write my debut book. That night I opened up my writing software, outlined the initial draft and began writing that book. I felt as if a dam of inspiration was released from my mind. I kept going back and forth to my book library looking for quotes to supplement my written thoughts. There, I retrieved books which I had previously read. I scanned through their pages, locating the exact high-lighted quote necessary for insert into the waiting text. I felt possessed with - the Michael Jordan like feeling when he dumped 69 points on the Cleveland Cavaliers. Inspiration took over.

Consequently, I passionately completed the first draft of that volume in one week.

An editor and cover designer stepped up to the plate as if summoned by some unknown guide. I must admit that I spoke with several designers over a three month span who promised to work with me on the project but never did. Finally, the right one showed up. He found exactly the image I was looking for and the book was published in June of 2007. I was ecstatic.

The book was subsequently released and made available on Amazon and at other online stores.

One of my clients, a well known celebrity who I chauffeured learned about my new book and promised to give me a "blurb" after reading its contents. She requested a copy. The book was delivered as requested. I waited for the blurb but never heard back from her. Nevertheless, my book received endorsements from other sources. Meanwhile my boss, who was her good friend, pulled the cord on me - I was out of a job. These turn of events was because someone couldn't see success for himself. Therefore, he didn't want it for me.

Later my roommate at the time said he didn't need the money but because of my velocity. I had taken so many of his excuses away during our dwelling together. See, while he slept, I wrote. Consequently, after weeks of unemployment I once more found myself homeless. The forces had again emerged. I was back sleeping in my car - A situation for which I was totally unprepared.

Back in 2007, while my editor edited my first book, I started writing Keep Love Alive. I later titled the volume Spread Some Love (Relationships 101) in order to cover the basics on relationships. MLK day the next year (2008) rolled around, and I was once again haunted by my lack of accomplishments in life thus far. In spite of my recurring adversity, on MLK day of 2008 I printed out the first completed draft of that book. With all the time management skills, I'd gleaned through the years. Without inspiration, I don't know if I could have pulled that off. Inspiration led me to action once again, and I created my own break instead of sitting around looking for it. I felt like I was born to write.

In early April that year founded my own publishing company "Books That Will Enhance Your Life." I published the Amazon kindle edition of the book. A few weeks later the e-book and paperback versions were published and released thereafter.

Upon receiving the proof of Spread Some Love - Relationships 101. I kissed it several times. A friend was with me at the time and jokingly said, "You kissed yourself" For those of you who have seen the book. You will notice that I've used one of my headshots on the front cover. To him, I replied "yes." If only he knew how much value I saw in this product. I knew that I had brought something of significance to the world.

A particular bookstore chain refused from stocking my book on their shelves. They flat out said "we are not going to carry that title because the author published it through a small independent publisher" and additionally "it didn't fit our model." That ticked me off because (a) I founded and owned that publishing company Books That Will Enhance Your Life and (b) I wrote the book in addition to owning the rights to it. That didn't sit too well with me, so I went undercover.

Their booksellers claimed that it was not modeled for their store. Well, based on my research, I found out that if a store really wanted to carry a book as long as it was available from one of the major distributors and was returnable. They could shortlist that book. However, instead they were saying flat out that they were not going to carry the title, "why?" I pried further.

By this time, I had refused from taking their "no" for an answer. In less than three weeks after doing my research and going on a tirade with them, they stocked my book in several of their California bookstores. That led to more stores following suit on the East Coast. When someone said no I purposefully pushed for the YES and got it.

Through Word Of Mouth marketing my book had already arrived on the shelves not only in

California but also on the East coast as well. So much that the constant flow of orders from that particular title alerted their corporate office according to their spokesperson. My sub publisher contacted me to make sure there had not been any fraud involved.

As far as I knew people were just flat out ordering copies of the book. My phone line was burning up with inquiries about this new title. Friends were telling other friends about it just like a good movie. WOM marketing had the advantage. The small press acquisition department for that book chain dragged their feet with my title submission for national distribution. In the meantime, I'd already secured my first major book-signing event with one of their local stores.

The upcoming book signing was creating such a buzz, so much that a major entertainment TV station proposed to cover me along with the event. However, they pulled out one day before the event. They claimed that they weren't able to get a host interviewer to cover for that weekend. I immediately got on the phone and organized my own camera crew. Even a freelance stylist provided her services on my behalf.

The day arrived. I showed up excited and dressed to the nines, after all it was my first major book signing event. All eyes focused on me. The very inspirational on-camera interview ended, and then it was on to the book-signing event. In less than a few hours all the books they had in stock were sold out much to the surprise of their management team. Their cash registers were going from Cha Ching – Cha Ching - Cha Ching. I watched as "Spread Some Love - Relationships 101" exited in shopping bags.

Those results still did not influence the small press into a nationwide - in - store placement of the volume. They came up with every worn out excuse under the sun, including me possibly trying a later resubmission of the title.

While they were dealing with indecision at that department surrounding acquisition of my book, the visionary mindset in me operated at the full throttle. I was busy creating the script for a docu-drama based on the book. The volume had heretofore sold thousands of copies without any major publicity within the first four months. It was so far apparent to me that people were hungry relationally. Therefore, no matter how long the current recession lasted. I knew that relationship minded individuals were still going to be working on their relationships.

A WORKBOOK version based on the same title, the 52 week JOURNAL PLUS, as well as the

SOUNDTRACK from the docu-drama has just been released. In a few weeks "The FIREPACE INTERVIEW" – a steamy interview about relation-ships between men and women will become available. MEMOIRS, a book based on reactions and life transformations pursuant to the Spread Some Love - Relationships 101 Series will be released in the fall. While a reality show based on that concept along with radio and other TV shows are currently in development. In addition, several new books are already in the pipeline, plus a movie based on my Hollywood Story.

While beating the odds, I squeezed $50,000.00 out of my pocket and despite non-supporting individuals who initially said that they'd participate but reneged during pre-production, the camera rolled. My former improvisation acting coach had already said yes too helming the project as his directorial debut. I was also busily conducting the dialog with some proposed members of the cast whose commitments were forthcoming. Some of the cast chickened out later. Even so, I was confident about what I had my hands on.

The first day on the set was very emotional. There were no dry eyes, including the cast and crew alike. True love had hit to the very core, validating that I had a great project. From much adversity had come forth "GOOD."

IT COULDN'T BE DONE

Somebody said it couldn't be done,

But he with a chuckle replied

That "maybe it couldn't," but he would be one

Who wouldn't say till he'd tried,

So he buckled right in with the trace of a grin

On his face. If he worried, he'd hid it.

Somebody scoffed: "Oh, you'll never do that;

At least no one ever has done it.

But he took off his coat and he took off his hat,

And the first thing we know he begun it.

With a lift of his chin and a bit of a grin,

Without any doubting or quiddit,

He started to sing as he tackled the thing

That couldn't be done, and he did it.

There are thousands to tell you it cannot be done,

There are thousands to prophesy failure;

There are thousands to point out to you one by one;

The dangers that wait to assail you.

But just buckle in with a bit of a grin,

Just take off your coat and go to it

Just start in to sing as you tackle the thing

That "cannot be done" and you'll do it.

--Unknown

In The 5 Steps To Changing Your Life, I recounted the persistency of one of America's biggest failures. It would have been so easy for this young man to bow his head in shame and give up. He failed in business in 1831, he was defeated for the legislature in '32, he was elected to the legislature in '34, his sweetheart died in '35, he had a nervous breakdown in '36, he was defeated for Speaker in '38, he was defeated for elector in '40, he was defeated for Congress in '43, he was elected to Congress in '48, he was defeated for the Senate in '50, and he was defeated for Vice President in '56 and for the Senate in '58. But in 1860, he was elected

President of the United States. His name was Abraham Lincoln.[4]

You will find inevitably that most successful people have all encountered failure along their path. Some of them experienced failure many times, others hundreds of times, while some ranked as high as in the thousands of times – as in the case of Thomas A. Edison. The most important element in their accomplishment is that they never gave up.

Any successful person will tell you that it takes hard work and strong character to succeed. And this goes for all area of their lives. A number of years ago after my divorce, I got immersed into the subject of relationships and have written many books on the subject. I've noticed that many people work hard on their jobs and not on their relationships. As a result they end up in divorce and wonder why their marriage hasn't worked. Determination starts with knowing that you have what it takes to succeed, and therefore, you are not going to be denied.

Are you ready for the climb amidst the turbulence in order to acquire success? How is your thought process?

If you *think* you are beaten, you are,

If you *think* you dare not, you don't.

If you like to win, but you *think* you can't,

It is almost certain you won't.

"If you *think* you'll lose, you are lost,

For out in this world we find,

Success begins with a fellow's will–

It's all in the *state of mind*.

"If you *think* you are outclassed, you are,

You've got to *think* high to rise,

You've got to *be sure of yourself* before

You can ever win a prize.

Life's battles don't always go

To the stronger or faster man,

But soon or late the man who wins

Is the man WHO THINKS HE CAN!

- Unknown

Not on your life do people get to experience the other 90% of their potential. They experience the thrill of sweet success without exhausting it.

On the other hand, nobody has ever accomplished anything worthwhile without being tested and tried. Successful people are winners; they let nothing stand in their way of victory. You can smell their tenacity like expensive cologne because they have a feeling of their own worth. They think: I can. I will and I shall not be denied.

The power of your purpose depends on the vigor and determination behind it. And your determination is necessary to take that ball into the end zone and score that touchdown.

First you have to believe, really believe that you can become successful before you do. "We do not attract that which we want but that which we are."[5] It has to be a mindset. And success is a process which takes patience. We live in a microwave age where everything is instantaneous. Immediately, you want this and right away you want that. Well, there is no such thing as instant success. Success is never like the "Jack and the Beanstalk scenario. It is the complete opposite.

Sometimes other people don't see what we do while we are in the trenches in order to acquire our success. Most times they only see the result and mistakenly call it luck.

I am always reminded of the growing of The Chinese Bamboo Tree whenever I think about determination. Success calls for great determination. Ask any success!

You take a little seed and plant, water, and fertilize it for a whole year, and nothing happens.

The second year you water and fertilize it, and nothing happens.

The third year you water and fertilize it, and nothing yet.

The fourth year you water and fertilize it, and still nothing.

The fifth year you continue to water and fertilize the seed. Sometime during the fifth year, the Chinese bamboo tree sprouts and grows NINETY FEET IN SIX WEEKS.

Most often success is like that Chinese Bamboo Tree, requiring you to hang in there much longer before seeing the fruits of your labor. Many misunderstand the process and view success like throwing on a superman outfit – such a temporary ordeal. Don't be mistaken, It goes much deeper than that. No wonder it becomes unnerving for most failures to be in the presence of the fortunate for far too long because that victorious person quickly takes their excuses away.

According to Malcolm Gladwell in his book Outliers "What is the question we always ask about the successful? We want to know what they're like –what kind of personalities they have, or how intelligent they are, or what kind of lifestyles they have, or what special talents they might have been born with. And we assume that it is those personal qualities that explain how that individual reached the top."6 He continues: "In the autobiographies published every year by the billionaire/entrepreneur/rock star/celebrity, the story line is always the same: our hero is born in modest circumstances and by virtue of his own grit and talent fights his way to greatness."7

Michael Phelps made it a habit of working out in the pool for 8 hours a day for several years in order to accomplish Olympic excellence.

We find that failure contributes greatly to one's success. Michael Jordan, the greatest player to play the game of basketball addressed failing this way, "I've missed more than 9,000 shots in my career, I've lost almost 300 games. Twenty six times I've been trusted to take the game winning shot and missed.

I've failed over and over and over in my life. And that's why I succeed!"

When we think of Michael Jordan, we remember him as "Air Jordan." Some of his stats: Six-time NBA champion (1991-93, 1996-98); MVP (1988, '91, '92, '96, '98); 10-time All-NBA First Team (1987-93, 1996-98) etc. Memories of his failures aren't foremost on our minds. We just remember his achievements. For most of us, we can still see him with his tongue hanging out as he took the ball to the hoop.

Despite being turned down by 403 banks while he embarked upon the quest of raising money to create Disneyland. Walt Disney succeeded, and has now brought illumination an adventure to the lives of so many kids and adults.

In grade school Albert Einstein was a very unimpressive student. So much that when his dad asked the headmaster what profession his young son should pursue, the headmaster replied, "It doesn't matter, because he will never make success in anything,"[9] The rest is historic. Einstein became one of the greatest physicists of the 20th century. His persistence developed in him the natural gifts of genius.

The Wright brothers, Orville and Wilbur wanted to construct a machine that flew. People believed that it was highly impossible. "How do you keep that thing up there? Never, it's impossible!" They questioned. In addition, while the two brothers were busily pursuing their invention, scientific studies were carried out to prove that a body heavier than air could not possibly fly. Because of their success, we now travel in an airplane for the duration of over twelve hours in the sky across several continents.

She was referred to as "Moses" not only by the hundreds of slaves she helped to freedom but also by the thousands of others she inspired. Because of her commitment to a cause Harriet Tubman became the most famous leader of the Underground Railroad to aid slaves escaping the Free states or Canada.

Born into slavery in Maryland, she escaped her own chains in 1849 to safety in Pennsylvania. A feat accomplished through the Underground Railroad, an elaborate and secret series of houses, tunnels, and roads set up by abolitionists and former slaves. "When I found I had crossed the [Mason-Dixon] line, I looked at my hands to see if I were the same person," Tubman later wrote. ". . . the sun came like gold through the tree and over the field and I felt like I was in heaven." She would spend the rest of her life helping other slaves escape to freedom.

After her escape, she worked as a maid in Philadelphia and joined the large and active abolitionist group in the city. In 1850, after Congress passed the Fugitive Slave Act, making it illegal to help a runaway slave, Tubman decided to join the Underground Railroad.

Her first expedition took place in 1851, when she managed to thread her way through the backwoods to Baltimore and return to the North with her sister and her sister's children. From that time until the onset of the Civil War, she traveled to the South about 18 times and helped close to 300 slaves escape. In 1857, led her parents to freedom in Auburn, New York, and resided there.

Tubman was never caught and never lost a slave to the Southern militia. As her reputation grew, so too did the desire among Southerners to put a stop to her activities. Rewards for her capture once totaled about $40,000, a lot of money in those days. During the Civil War, Tubman served as a nurse, scout, and sometime-spy for the Union army, mainly in South Carolina. She also took part in a military campaign that resulted in the rescue of 756 slaves and destroyed millions of dollars' worth of enemy property.

After the war, Tubman returned to Auburn and continued her involvement in social issues, including the women's rights movement. In 1908, she established a home in Auburn for elderly and indigent blacks that later became known as the Harriet Tubman Home. She died on March 10, 1913, at approximately age of 93.[10]

Tubman's passionate commitment of love for her people kept her going back until every slave was freed, regardless of the dangers involved.

The foregoing people are normal like you and me, though because of their uniqueness, they have acquired their unrivalled brand of success. Commonly, though, they have been driven by an extra-ordinary determination to achieve their individual goals at all costs. Every opposition brought them closer to a "YES." They are adept at turning setbacks into comebacks. Nothing in the world can take the place of persistence. Talent will not. Nothing is more common than unsuccessful men with talent. Genius will not. Unrewarded genius is almost a proverb. Education will not. The world is full of educated derelicts. Persistence, determination and hard work make the difference.[1]
– Calvin Coolidge.

Persistence is such a fitting word for determination. This special character trait ought to be embodied in the legacy we pass on to our kids. It's a common trend that kids tend to develop their relationship values from their parents. And those qualities they pass on to future generations.

A new bride was one day making dinner for her husband. He noticed that she cut off both ends of the ham before putting it in the saucepan. He was taken aback and asked: Why such a move? She responded that her mom always cut off the ends of the ham before cooking it, making it very delicious. One day while he was with her mother, he asked her why she cut off the ends of the ham before cooking it. She said she didn't know, and that she saw her mom doing it that way, and it was delicious. One day while with his wife's grandma he pried further about this ham cooking process. She said I cut the ends off my ham because it was too big to fit in my small roasting pan. It has nothing to do with the taste and texture. I had to cut the ends out of the ham to get it to fit in my pan!

So, just because someone else did it doesn't mean you should do it too because of tradition. Would you be the one to reconstruct your ancestral values thus creating a lineage of future champions?

Ask any successful person and they will tell you that going through those walls towards their destiny took persistence and strong determination to succeed. However, once they broke through, their life like that of the beautiful butterfly going through the cocoon became enhanced.

LIFE IS BIGGER THAN FOOTBALL OR BASKETBALL BUT THE SAME RULES MAINTAIN. IF YOU KEEP STRONG, PHYSICALLY FIT, FULL OF ENERGY AND ENTHUSIASM, YOU ARE THE MAN WHOM LIFE'S COACH IS GOING TO PICK WHEN THE WINNING TOUCHDOWN IS NEEDED.[1]

– WILLIAM DANFORTH.

Chapter Eight

BALANCE

Successful individuals deserve a well rounded life. After all, the price paid for success is very significant. Therefore, life should be enjoyed to the fullest. The mental, physical, social or spiritual area of life should not be neglected by anyone desiring success. The ones desiring a long life practice moderation in everything they do.

Learning to smell the roses along the way is of utmost importance for anyone wanting to be successful. Some people work all the time and find no time to play or do anything fun. I'm not talking about putting aside what needs to get done in order to succeed and devote that time towards having a great time. Many would-be-successes spend most of their time having a blast and wonder why they are not as successful as they can be.

On the other hand, some work all the time just because of the income potential and spend very little time working on their relationships. As a result, if married, that relationship collapses catapulting then into divorce court.

God created the world in 6 days and he took some time off to rest. I realize that he's a busy God, dealing with all of our issues. He's all powerful, not sure if he needs the rest but could it be that he's sending us a message to rest? Time spent for a rest, and spiritual input does well for our mind, body and soul. God made us and knows what we need in order to function at our full capacity. By rebelling, there always seem to be a detour along the way which will bring those of such a mindset back to Him in many different ways. Be it a health issue which serves as a reminder that we need to take care of us or some catastrophe, which reminds us that we are not in total control. Success demands a full price – there are absolutely no shortcuts.

The bible states that our bodies are the temple of God and what we put inside can defile it. By putting in the wrong diet on a consistent basis, those slight edge decisions come back to haunt us. Think about your automobile and instead of pouring motor oil into the crank case you poured a handful of dirt. How much longer would that vehicle be operable?

In order to maintain durable healthy bodies exercise is a high priority. If we want strength, we have to acquire strength necessary for a strong body. Exercise also serves as a means of releasing waste products from our bodies. It's ironic that we service our cars but become negligent about the upkeep of our bodies. According to Danforth: *Life is bigger than football or basketball but the same rules maintain. If you keep strong, physically fit, full of energy and enthusiasm, you are the man whom life's coach is going to pick when the winning touchdown is needed*.[1]

When we take care of the mental, physical, social and spiritual aspects of our lives, we are not only creating balance but showing our gratitude for being wonder-fully made and totally equipped to fulfill our destiny.

ANYONE WHO DOESN'T REALLY KNOW WHAT HE OR SHE WANTS TO DO AND DOESN'T ESTABLISH CLEAR-CUT GOALS WILL FIND IT HARD TO SUCCEED.[1]

- MARK FISHER

Chapter Nine

FULFILLING YOUR DESTINY

If you have gotten this far by now you should be totally equipped and fully loaded to set your sails toward your destiny. What is your port of call? Every ship has a destination. Could you imagine a ship wandering on the sea going nowhere? In order to get what you want you need to know what you want and go for it. Your destiny has nothing to do with other people's opinion. It has to do with you. Most people have an entitlement mindset. They not only think that the world owes them something but that the world, not them, needs to change.

Successful people not only ask themselves: Where do I want to go in my life and career but what do I want to become? Is your destiny well defined? I hope by now that you've found that "cause" greater than yourself and are ready to make it happen. In case you are still lacking a cause, you may want to read this book again before proceeding; repetition has proven to be a very important element of success.

We all have a divine untapped power, capable of guiding us towards fulfilling our destiny. Some, not yet successful may reason: Where is it? Why I've never experienced it? Do you believe in electricity? I remember growing up as a kid. In those early days, we didn't have electricity. When the power supply finally came to our area, I was in my late teens and like most boys with an experimental mindset decided to look for what I couldn't see – electricity. One day the perfect opportunity arose as the need to have light in our factory became apparent. So I decided to run an extension wire from our kitchen to the factory only a few yards away. I removed the screws from the light socket, looking inside there was no evidence of electricity just one black and one red wire However, when my hand inadvertently touched the red wire, my arm was almost pulled out of its socket a few times in a matter of seconds. I couldn't see the electricity, but you better believe it was there in that socket. Evidence of success seems to lack in our lives.

Mainly, because our destiny has not been defined. Consequently, we are not en-route because we don't know where we are going pursuant to the lack of self-knowledge.

When you know who you are, you would realize that you have within the power to become the co-creator of your entire world. Let me explain. Self knowledge is your power. When the newly discovered you emerge, you are able to manage the circumstances of your life more readily. Your image of self becomes enhanced; you step out of your comfort zone and into the game of life. You see what you lack and begin to participate in your reconstruction process.

Ask any successful person and they will tell you there was a point right after their self discovery process. They knew beyond a shadow of a doubt. They were going to become successful. They will also tell you that once they became focused on their destiny, they refused to let any powers within them lie dormant. They dug it up and operated on the full throttle. At that point, they knew where they wanted to go in life. They had found their destiny – their true calling.

Successful people understand the law of momentum, knowing that it's hard to acquire but easy to lose. So whenever this awesome force is present they use it to accomplish their quantum leap. Thereby, they became unstoppable in the eyes of many.

Yes "We are powerful beyond measure." How do we know that? We know through self discovery. When self is discovered, we move beyond our limitations, and as a result we become unstoppable towards fulfilling our destiny. The detours along the way become minuscule because we've learned to trust ourselves and our creator. And because of our faith we are able to turn our defeats into victory.

Each of us has a destiny to fulfill, and it's up to us if we reject or accept that calling. When God gave us a "cause" he also placed hidden guides along the way to assist us on that journey. Have you ever been on the road to a destination, got lost, and immediately found someone placed in your path as if by design to help you get back on the right track? However, most of us lack the ability to start because we're not sure we'll arrive. Each of us has a calling. What you do with your calling is largely dependable on your commitment to completing life's puzzle. You could be holding on to that missing piece. We all are workers together with our Maker. He wants to bless us abundantly. All he requires of us is to make this world a better place.

And by contributing, he opens the floodgates, pour blessing down upon us. He says that "The cattle on a thousand hills belong to him" and he is willing to share a part of that herd with us. However, we have to earn it. We first need to prove that we deserve it by bringing value to the world. He gave us life. What we do with our lives determines the value of the gift, we give back to him. Mark Fisher writes in the book: How to be a Millionaire Anyone who doesn't really know what he or she wants to do and doesn't establish clear-cut goals will find it hard to succeed.[49]

Our contribution is imperative in order to make this world a better place. When our journey here is ended would it be one, which served as a blessing to humanity? Alternatively, would it be one that your grand children don't even remember your name, or no one benefits because you came. In the words of Ralph Waldo Emerson "Do not go where the path may lead, go instead where there is no path and leave a trail."[2]

Self made millionaire T. Harv Eker who went from zero to a millionaire in only two and a half years, writes in his book *Secrets of The Millionaire Mind* "Becoming rich isn't as much about getting rich financially as about whom you have become, in character and mind, to get rich."[3] He further states,

"The fastest way to get rich and stay rich is to work on developing *you!* The idea is to grow yourself into a 'successful' person. Again your outer world is merely a reflection of your inner world. You are the root; your results are the fruits."[4]

Earl Nightingale was born during economically depressed times. As a child because they were so poor Earl desperately wanted to know why some people grew up to enjoy prosperity. While, others, like his family struggled merely to survive. Unable to find answers to his questions from grown ups, he began reading everything he could believing that someone, somewhere had the answer.

When Earl was 35 years old he'd written and record a message. It was to be played one Saturday morning to a small group of salespeople during his absence. When Earl returned he learned that the message had made such a positive impact on the men, they wanted copies to share with their friends and families. He arranged with Columbia records to duplicate the record to meet their many requests. Much to his surprise in very little time, without any real advertising or marketing, over a million copies have been sold and he received a gold record. Earl called the message "The Strangest Secret." And this single recording was the seedling from which the entire personal development industry grew. And because he had discovered the true meaning of The

Strangest Secret, which determines the outcome of one's life, he went from poverty to become one of the most highly recognized voices and name throughout the United States and from the West Indies to South Africa.

People around the world have attributed The Strangest Secret as the one message which has positively affected their lives.[5]

Many people, failing to discover themselves go to their grave with their music unleashed. We mourn their death – a great lost. Conversely, we overlook the fact that the greatest squander is what died in many of us while we are yet still alive. What will happen if you were to release the brakes on our potential? The world would not only experience a scientific revolution but a cultural and financial one as well. The record high unemployment rate no doubt speedily experiences a decline.

Notes

23. Marianne Williamson
http://thinkexist.com/quotation/as_we_let_our_li
ght_shine-we_consciously_give/341050.html

Introduction

23. Martin Luther King Jr.
www.brainyquote.com/quotes/m/martinluth1150
56.html
24. Ibid. dontknowmuch.com/kids/mlk.html
25. Harland Stoncipher, Pre-Paid Legal Services.
Inc.
26. Oprah Winfrey – Bio
www.answers.com/topic/oprah-winfrey
27. Philip & Holly Wagner. 2009, Oasisla.org

Chapter 1

1. William Danforth, *I Dare You* (St. Louis:
American Youth Foundation, 1991), X.
27. Gerald Sindell, The Genius Machine, Novato,
New World Library, 2009), 66
28. Warren Bennis, *On Becoming a Leader,* Inc.
Ontario & New York, Addison-Wesley Publishing
Company, 19890, 54

Chapter 2

28. Ken Blanchard, Leading At A Higher Level, Prentice Hall, New Jersey, 2007, 280

29. Rick Warren, The Purpose Driven Life, Grand Rapids, Zondervan, 2002), 319

30. Napoleon Hill, The Master Key To Riches/Your Magic Power To Be Rich, New York, Penguin Group, 2007), 363

31. James Allen, *As a Man Thinketh* (New York: Bantam Books Inc., 1982),

32. Julia Cameron, The Artist's Way, New York, Tatcher/Putman. 1992), 66

33. Ibid. 66

34. Mark Fisher/Marc Allen, How To Think Like A Millionaire, Novato, New World Library, 1997), 72 (Ibid)

35. Colonel Sanders.
www.articlesbase.com/entrepreneurship-articles/colonel-sanders-story-of-entrepreneurship-1000394.html

36. J.Paul Getty. www.zeromillion.com/srs-j-paul-getty

Chapter 3

36. Philip Baker, *Secret of Super Achievers* (New Kensington: Whitaker House, 2005), 77

37. William Danforth, I Dare You, 5

38. Bill Gates'-
Bio.http://Inventors.about.com/od/gstartinventors/a./Bill_gates.html

39. Rosa Parks. Live My Passion,
- http://www.livemypassion.com/thoughts.htm

Chapter 4

39. John Maxwell, Becoming A Person Of Influence, Nashville, Thomas Nelson Publis-hers, 1997), 7
40. Brian Tracy, Millionaire Habits, Entrepreneur Press, 2006) xi, xii
41. Ibid. 196

Chapter 5

41.BrainyQuote.
www.brainyquote.com/quotes/quotes/j/johnfken n132742.html
42. Mark Fisher/Marc Allen, How To Think Like A Millionaire, 64
43. Ken Blanchard, Leading At A Higher Level, 25
44. Ibid, 22
45. Mark Fisher/Marc Allen, How To Think Like A Millionaire, 71
46. Howard Schultz's Bio.
www.myprimetime.com/work/ge/shultzbio/
47. Ken Blanchard, Leading At A Higher Level, 25
48. Chris Gardener – Bio.
http://www.evancarmichael.com/Famous-Entrepreneurs/815/Chris-Gardner-Bio.html

9. Allen, *As a Man Thinketh*, revision. JMW Group Inc. New York, Published by Penguin Group, 2008), 110.

10. Ibid, 110

11. Life of Dr. King, www.webstar.co.uk/~ubugaje/**luther**3.html

12. Allen, *As a Man Thinketh*, 40,41

Chapter 6

12.1.1. Malcom Gladwell, The Tipping Point, New York/Boston, Back Bay Books, 2000), 258

12.1.2. Benjamin Disraeli. www.brainyquote.com/quotes/b/benjamindi1343 31.html

12.1.3. Abraham Lincoln .www.brainyquote.com/quotes/a/abrahamlin1092 75.html

12.1.4. Robert kiyosaki, Rich Dad Poor Dad, New York/Boston, Business Plus, Hachette Book Group, 1997), 126

12.1.5. Ibid, 126

12.1.6. Ibid, 125

12.1.7. James Allen, As A Man Thinketh, 41

12.1.8. Napoleon Hill, Law of Success, Los Angeles, High Roads Media, 2004), 572

Chapter 7

12. Skip Ross with Carole C. Carlson, *Say Yes to Your Potential* (Rockford, MI: Circle "A" Productions, 1983), 145, 146

13. Napoleon Hill, *Think and Grow Rich* (Chatsworth: Wilshire Book Company, 1999), 16

14. Martin Luther King Jr. UBR, Inc., The American, The New Business Magazine For People Who Think. -- http://www.people.ubr.com/

15. Abraham Lincoln, Alan Loy McGinnis, *Bringing Out the Best in People* (Minneapolis: Augsburg Publishing House, 1985), 76.

16. James Allen, 13

17. Malcolm Gladwell, Outliers, New York, Hachette Book Group, 2008), 18

18. Ibid. 18

19. Jordan. htpp://quotations.about.com/od/stillmorefamous people/a/michaeljoradan1.html

20. Einstein. http://www.essortment.com/all/biographyofein_r wdi.htm

21. The Civil War Society's "Encyclopedia of the Civil War" http://www.civilwarhome.com/tubmanbio.htm

Chapter 8

21. Danforth. I Dare You, 26

Chapter 9

21. Mark Fisher/Marc Allen, 107

22. Think Like A Champion, New York, Vanguard Press, 2009), 147

23. T. Harv Eker, Secrets of the Millionaire Mind, New York, Collins Business, 2005), 183

24. Ibid, 183

25. Diana Nightingales' Intro, The Strangest Secret. Strangest Secret Millenium 2000 Gold Recording Audio CD. Earl Nightingale.

ABOUT THE AUTHOR

Prolific, national bestselling author, John A. Andrews was born in the Islands of St. Vincent and the Grenadines. He grew up in a home of five sisters and three brothers. His parents were all about values: work hard, love God and never give up on dreams. As a high school dropout John developed an interest for music. Although lacking the formal education he later put his knowledge and passion to good use, moonlighting as a disc jockey in New York. This paved the way for further exploration in the entertainment world. John's acting career began in 1994. Leaving the Big Apple for Los Angeles in 1997, not only put several national TV commercials under his belt but helped him to find his niche.

His passion for writing started in 2002 years ago when he was denied the rights to a 1970's classic film, which he so badly wanted to remake. In 2007, with two of his original screenplays in the development phase, he published his first book "The 5 Steps to Changing Your Life" He has just released a docu-drama based on his second book "Spread Some Love (Relationships 101)" which he wrote and produced. As an entrepreneur Mr. Andrews has published his last 5 books within the last year. He's currently publishing his seventh book.

DARE TO MAKE A DIFFERENCE – SUCCESS 101 FOR TEENS

Dare to Make a Difference - Success 101 For Teens is rich and full of history. Saturated, with stories about high achievers, who have daringly blazed the trails of success. Their chronicles are arranged buffet style, with something for everyone. Some accounts are short, funny, witty, thrilling, long, dramatic, daring, and to the point. Most of all they lend support to anyone bent on success.

SUCCESS 101

The Teacher's Guide

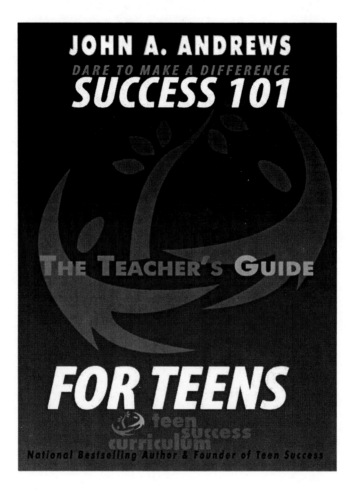

The FIVE "Ps" For Teens

The 5 Traits every teen should know and have.

CONTACT INFORMATION

For more information about *JOHN A. ANDREWS*, to book speaking engagements, sign up for his mailings, purchase his books and to learn more about other BOOKS THAT WILL ENHANCE YOUR LIFE ™, visit:

www. BooksThatWillEnhanceYourLife.com
EMAIL
john@booksthatwillenhanceyourlife.com

BOOKS THAT WILL ENHANCE YOUR LIFE™

CPSIA information can be obtained at www.ICGtesting.com
Printed in the USA
BVOW051020021011

272625BV00005B/58/P